Anxo Quintela
Jordi Puig

SANTIAGO
DE COMPOSTELA

TRIANGLE▼POSTALS

Santiago de Compostela
Summary

Santiago de Compostela
The Way

The first thing that changes when one begins a long journey Is not the landscape, but time. Getting moving is also, paradoxically, halting the lineal succession of the hours and days to enter into a new time dimension, that which marks the rhythm and cadence of what is walked. As in the river of Heraclites, nobody goes along the same path twice. Neither does the Saint James Way.

For those that do it for religious reasons it is the time for prayer and conversion. For all pilgrims, however, whatever the reason for their journey, day-to-day time stops and a new time scale opens: that of the stages, the tiredness, the silence and encounters.

Why go to Santiago? Why this long way to what in another time was the end of the world? The phenomenon of pilgrimages is common in nearly all religions and eras. This nomadic character is inscribed in the cultural DNA of humanity. Massive pilgrimages are documented as much as 2000 years before Christ to sacred spots in Babylonia, and the great oriental religions, from Hinduism to Buddhism, devote a great deal of time to reflecting on and practicing pilgrimage. In the Christian world, the Roman emperor Constantine promoted pilgrimages to the holy places of Jerusalem in the 4th century. Years later, in the 7th century, the phenomenon of pilgrimages experienced a notable growth throughout Europe, especially in the territory of the Franks. The Church called upon believers to go en masse to places where the relics of saints and martyrs were venerated. Small pilgrimage routes criss-crossed the western world. This was the setting when in the 9th century the discovery was announced all over Europe, in a remote spot of faraway Gallaecia, of the sepulchre of the apostle Saint James. The news did not have the initial impact that perhaps it deserved. However, over a period of two hundred years the Saint James Way became established as one of the three routes of pilgrimage, along with Rome and Jerusalem, of the Christian West. The many sanctuaries spread around Europe became stages of the three great routes.

Beyond the myth

Throughout the Middle Ages the Saint James Way became a complex phenomenon that transcends what is purely religious. It was a journey there and back, of penetration and cultural and economic exchange. Along the way travelled kings and queens, troubadours, men and women of arts and science, artists, adventurers, bandits, traders, bishops and monks; and with them came goods and knowledge. The universal nature of the pilgrimage to Santiago is shown, for example, in a large number of *lenguajeros* who lived in Santiago. They were translators employed to make intelligible to the confessors the tales of penitents who came from all over Europe.

The French Way produced new routes from all the cardinal points, both from land and sea. Many pilgrims continued the journey to Fisterra, thus recreating a supposed and remote route to the end of the known world. At the same time, Santiago acquired new appearances: that of the pilgrim, with their scallop shell, cape and hat, or that of the warrior, who came on horseback in rescue of the Christian troops in the Battle of Clavijo. The call for the intervention of the apostle in this legendary battle by the Compostela Church became one of its main sources of income for centuries. The Vow of Santiago obliged the peasants from an enormous territory, between Galicia and La Rioja, to pay a tax directly to the Archbishop of Compostela. It was abolished in the Cortes de Cádiz, in the early 19th century.

The Codex Calixtinus

The arts of Archbishop Diego Gelmírez turned Compostela into a place of mass pilgrimages in the 12th century. The increasingly greater influence of pilgrims and the growing fame of the Way created the need to satisfy their expectations, both spiritual and material. It was during this period, in the mid-12th century, when the first pilgrim's guide was written, the fifth of the five books that form the famous, for different reasons, Codex Calixtinus.

Rúa das Casas Reais

It is almost miraculous that after the vicissitudes it suffered throughout history (the latest, its disappearance due to robbery for a year wrapped in a plastic bag in the junk room of a garage) it has reached us today practically intact. Pope Calixtus himself stated in the introductory text of the book: "On my travels through foreign lands to produce the Codex I fell into the hands of thieves, and stripped of everything, I was only left with the manuscript. I was a prisoner in prisons and lost all my property, left only with the manuscript. A house in which I was staying burnt down and my belongings perished, but the manuscript did not burn. For this reason I reached the conclusion that this codex that I wanted to undertake with my hands was thanks to God."

A living city

On arriving in Compostela you will find a city specialised for centuries in welcoming and caring for the traveller. You will no doubt want to quickly visit the Cathedral, because this building is the key and central axis of Compostela history. In fact, in some ways the city is an emanation of it: it managed to create life revolving around a sepulchre. And this continues to be one of the main characteristics of the old quarter of Santiago: it is not an empty setting filled only with art and history, but an inhabited city. It is the universal city that welcomes you.

Welcome centre for pilgrims, in the Rúa do Vilar

Steps of the Obradoiro   The Pilgrims Cross, Fisterra

Santiago de Compostela
The city

Compostela before Saint James

Compostela was founded on the edge of a way. As if its origin prefigured its destiny, the first evidence of human activity in today's city centre comes from the remains of a Roman mansion placed at the foot of Via XIX, which joined Braga with Astorga, passing through Lugo, the three main towns of Roman Gallaecia. Compostela emerged as a resting and supply spot, the "mansio Asseconia". The enclave occupied approximately one hectare around the land where today stands the Cathedral, and was already inhabited in the first century AD. Among the early constructions featured a mausoleum built with blocks of granite in the middle of a necropolis close to the way. The remains of the old funerary structure can be seen below the main altar of the Cathedral, in the space that the crypt of the sepulchre of Saint James now occupies. The coincidences do not end there, however. The outline of the Via XIX already announced the French Way: in the first settlement it entered via the current Rúa do Franco, and left via the Rúa de San Pedro. A way and a sepulchre: the two elements that define the history of Santiago de Compostela shape it from its inception.

A city around a sepulchre

During the first five centuries BC, the necropolis gradually occupied more space in the city. In the 5th century there are no signs of human activity in the enclave. Between the 6th and 8th centuries Compostela was, it seems exclusively, a necropolis, a space for funerary use. Until in the 9th century, Teodomiro, the Bishop of Iria Flavia, and King Alfonso II announced the

Avenida de Raxoi

Santiago from the hilltop of Pedroso >

discovery of the sepulchre of the apostle Saint James. Despite the relevance of the finding, what we would today call the first urban developments around the tomb of Saint James were not very ambitious. A modest church was built in stone and clay over the mausoleum of the apostle, as well as the episcopal residence and the early church and monastery of Anteataltares to house a small monastic community. At the beginning of the 10th century, under the reign of Alfonso III and with Sisnando in the episcopal see of Iria, the place took on a greater degree of splendour. The second large basilica of Santiago was raised, now with marble and other fine materials, and around it, new churches and monasteries, such as that of Santo Estevo de Pinario, predecessor of the actual San Martiño Pinario, the city wall in stone and the first lodging for the pilgrims. The current Rúas do Vilar and do Franco and the Praza de Cervantes were already mapped out in the Compostela of the early 10th century. This first show of prosperity would be broken on the 10th of August 997. The troops of Al-Mansur razed a deserted city, even destroying the basilica of the apostle but, according to tradition, respected the sepulchre. Santiago stopped being a modest sanctuary of the old Gallaecia to become a tempting spot for robbery. Compostela now gave its name to a whole territory: Jacobsland.

The medieval splendour

Bishop Pedro de Mezonzo, who ordered the evacuation of the city before the threat of Al-Mansur, also led its reconstruction. In the 11th century a large defensive wall was completed with its corresponding gateways: the Porta Faxeira, that of Mazarelos or Da Pena, which we can identify on the street map of the city today. The construction of the Romanesque cathedral also began in this period. The city grew at the same rate as the flow of pilgrims. The bishop —by now archbishop— Diego Gelmírez was able to carry out, among other projects, the biggest urban development plan that Compostela had ever experienced until then. The pilgrims arrived in even greater numbers, and new infrastructures were absolutely essential: an aqueduct was built, new streets opened, for example Rúa Nova parallel to Rúa del Vilar; a Pilgrims' Hospital was created; new churches and monasteries were erected, such as that of Sar; trade was regulated in the city, a marketplace established, today's Praza de Cervantes. Meanwhile, the construction of the grand cathedral progressed. At the end of the Middle Ages, Compostela was home to a population of 5,000 people.

The Baroque, enlightened and modern Compostela

Gelmírez drew up the fundamental traits of the city: the main streets, the squares and some of the most significant buildings. The urban appearance, however, was very different to what we see today. The majority of dwellings were made of wood, of a single storey, a long way from the Santiago built in stone. In the 16th century the Hospital Real, the Hostal de los Reyes Católicos, and on the other side of the square, the Colegio de Fonseca, the main centre of the future university, were all built. New colleges were built: that of San Clemente and that of Las Orfas, and new works were undertaken in the cathedral. The 17th century constituted a new age of splendour: Compostela vindicated itself before the world through Baroque style. In a period of decadence of the pilgrimages, new constructions were undertaken that transformed the appearance of the city: the Clock Tower of the Cathedral was built and civil construction was given a boost: Casa da Parra or Casa da Conga in the Praza da Quintana are some examples. But the image of Santiago, the one we all have in our minds, would not be revealed until the 18th century, when the construction of the Obradoiro façade of the Cathedral was completed. The church, the university and small aristocracy of rural landowners conditioned the urban dynamics of Santiago in the most important part of its history, from the university campus to the infrastructure for receiving the pilgrims. In recent years, since Santiago de Compostela became the capital of Galicia and headquarters for the autonomous government, the uniform face of the city has become more nuanced and plural. At the end of a way, around a sepulchre. Just like 2,000 years ago.

Viewpoint of the Árbol,
park of La Alameda

Hejduk Towers,
Cidade da Cultura

1   The Cathedral and its setting

Compostela can be understood as a succession of concentric circles, like the shape of a large scallop shell or a superimposition of two geometric shapes: the spiral and the star. However, in any case, the axis, not the centre, is occupied by the Cathedral: the driving force of the urban dynamism of Santiago throughout almost the entire history of the city. As if projected through a kaleidoscope, four squares surround the temple. Each one has its own character: the Obradoiro, which opens the main façade and synthesises the character of the city; Praterías, which appears as a small Baroque stage overlooked by the Romanesque façade and the Clock Tower; Quintana, where the moon dances, according to the poem in Galician by Federico García Lorca, and the Praza da Acibechería, which is entered by the Puerta del Paraíso. A route along the different expressions of the genius of stone that Santiago de Compostela carved throughout the centuries.

1
Cathedral of Santiago

2
The Cathedral Museum

3
Hostal de los Reyes Católicos

4
Pazo de Raxoi

5
Gelmírez Palace

6
College of San Xerome

7
College of Fonseca

8
Convent of
San Francisco

9
Church of
San Fructuoso

10
Monastery of
San Martiño Pinario

11
Convent of San Paio
de Antealtares

12
Casa del Deán

13
Casa do Cabido

14
Casa da Parra

15
Casa da Conga

Praza do Obradoiro

You just need to stand in the middle and turn around to get an almost complete image of the history and meaning of Santiago de Compostela. The Praza do Obradoiro condenses the four pillars of the city. Like the four primordial elements of ancient times, air, earth, water and fire, in the Praza do Obradoiro faith, power, assistance and wisdom are present in their corresponding buildings: the Cathedral, the Pazo de Raxoi, the Hostal de los Reyes Católicos and the Colegio de San Xerome, home to the university vice-chancellor's office. The square has not always had the same name, which evokes the workshops of the stonemasons and builders who worked on the construction of the Cathedral. It was also Praza da Trindade, de la Constitución, Maior or de España. It is the main setting for official ceremonies and popular festivals: from the annual Offering to the Apostle to the spectacular firework display the night before the 25th of July, the festival of Saint James, Santiago.

Praza do Obradoiro

The Cathedral of Santiago

The Obradoiro Façade

The dimensions of the Cathedral, the richness and variety of its rooms and details and, on occasions, the labyrinthine nature of the tour, enable us to make a visit as if it were not so much a building but more a small city. An interior city with its historic centre, long avenues, secret alleyways, grand monuments, discrete homes and peculiar inhabitants.

The crypt of the apostle, the mausoleum that according to tradition guards the sarcophagus with the remains of Saint Zebedee and his two disciples Athanasius and Theodor, would form the old quarter in this imagined city. In the early 9th century, from the apostolic sepulchre, Alfonso II and Teodomiro built a modest church of just a single nave with ashlar walls. The king and the bishop placed here the first stones of what would be, in an almost uninterrupted construction process, reforms, rebuilding and extension, the current Cathedral of Santiago.

The early temple was succeeded shortly after by another of pre-Romanesque style, of basilica ground plan, more in line with the relevance of the discovery. Around this time, in the 10th century, one of the most singular "districts" of the cathedral city was also built: the chapel of the Corticela, in that period located on the periphery of the church of Santiago. Bishop Pedro de Mezonzo rebuilt the devastated building after the attack by the troops of Al-Mansur, but was soon too small to house the growing number of pilgrims who came to visit the spot.

Saint James the Apostle, main altar

The long "avenues" of the Cathedral, the three naves we now see, with their thick columns and elegant capitals, the main altar, the chapels of the ambulatory… a large part of the ground plan of the current Cathedral was designed and built between the end of the 11th century and all throughout the 12th. It was the period of Archbishop Gelmírez, the years in which the Romanesque porticoes of Praterías and Acibechería were built and, above all, the remarkable Glory Portico, the most important work of Master Mateo. We know hardly anything more about the great craftsman of European Romanesque sculpture than his name, except that he directed the works of the Glory Portico and the old stone choir of the Cathedral and lived comfortably thanks to a pension awarded to him by King Fernando II.

From the roofing to the excavated subsoil, from the Holy Door to the crypt and Royal Pantheon, from the steps of the Obradoiro to the bells in the Clock Tower, the Cathedral of Santiago is like a sediment of stone decanted over the years. After the period of Gelmírez, in the Middle Ages, came the 18th century, the age of Baroque splendour of the city, which left a greater stamp on the architectural constructions. The façade of the Obradoiro and the main chapel were built, the organs of the central nave installed and the exterior of the cathedral complex was completed. Then in the 19th century the new façade of the Acibechería was inaugurated.

Sacristy door

The Compostela cathedral, the small city that begot a city, sums up two thousand years of history; witness to and keeper of legends, faith, ambitions and ideals, a conjunction of architectural styles and living site of the traffic of thousands of pilgrims. Consecrated as a cathedral on the 21st of April 1211 by Archbishop Pedro Muñiz, the commemoration of the 800th anniversary brought together more than 200 people in a symbolic embrace. The Compostela basilica was declared a Cultural Interest Site at the end of the 19th century. Built in stone, iron and wood, it is also supported by the material of faith and dreams.

Organ of the Cathedral

Botafumeiro thurible, Chapter Library, Cathedral Museum

The Obradoiro façade

The main façade of the Cathedral rises above the Praza do Obradoiro, much higher than the other buildings with which it shares the space. No other is capable of putting it in the shade. Above all when it reflects the golden light of the dusk and the other constructions in the square enter into the semi-darkness. We can only imagine what the western entrance to the Cathedral would have been like before the construction, in the mid-18th century, of the current Baroque façade, work of the architect Fernando de Casas y Novoa. For six-hundred years the Cathedral was entered by some steps that led directly to the Glory Doorway, open to the square.

Stairway of the Obradoiro

Saint James Apostle

Saint Susana and Saint John, Tower of the Carraca >

The crypt of the Glory Portico

Nothing is stable enough without a good foundation. The entire western side of the Cathedral and Glory Portico are supported by the compact basement of the crypt. Located beneath the stairway of the entrance by Praza do Obradoiro, it was built by Master Mateo in the 12th century. Known as the "old cathedral", it is structured by means of cross vaulting, a technical innovation of the period.

Detail of
the tympanum

Glory Portico

The Glory Portico is one of the great representations of the medieval Christian world vision. The work by Master Mateo provides us with a vision of a universe ordered around the figure of Christ. It is an extremely powerful arrangement in stone in which the figures of prophets, apostles and some mysterious women seem to be talking to each other, giving the whole a serene dynamism. The enigmatic smile of the prophet Daniel synthesises the experience of contemplating the Portico.

Saint James Apostle,
Glory Portico

A The Glory · Final destination

B Limbo · The Jewish people wait

C The Final Judgement

D Prophets and apostles

E Animals

F Santo dos Croques. Possible representation by Master Mateo

1 The 24 elders of the Apocalypse

2 The just with white tunics

3 Christ resurrected

4 Saint John

5 Saint Lucas

6 Saint Matthew

7 San Marcos

8 Angel with the column of whips

9 Angels with the cross

10 Angel with the crown of thorns

11 Angel with the nails and the spear

12 Sentence of the condemned and vase

13 Whips

14 Spear and sponge

15 Tribes of Israel

16 Christ in Limbo between Adam and Eve and other figures of the Hebrew people

17 The blessed

18 Heads of Christ and Saint Michael

19 The just taken by the angels

20 The Final Judgement · The Condemned

21 The glutton and the drinker

22 The just with angels

23 · 24 · 25 Prophets of the Old Testament

26 · 27 · 28 Apostles

29 Mythical hero fighting two lions

30 Tree of Jesse

31 The Trinity

32 Saint James Apostle

1   5

11   12   13   25

Dome

The central nave

The dimensions of the central nave make the Cathedral of Santiago the largest Romanesque temple on the Iberian Peninsula. On passing through the Glory Portico, the visitor stands before the view of the main altar, at the end of the nave. It was not always like this, though: in the Middle Ages, the central part of the ground plan was occupied by a large stone choir built by Master Mateo.

Main Chapel

The statue of a saint is either admired or prayed to, but very seldom hugged.
One of the most popular rites of a visit to the Cathedral consists of embrac-
ing the image of Saint James that overlooks the main altar. It is a sculpture
from the 13th century of the apostle with the cloak of the pilgrim: a setting that envelops an everyday gesture, a simple embrace.

Baldachin and Main Altar
of the Cathedral

The sepulchral crypt

The raison d'être of the Cathedral and the ways occupy a small silver urn beneath the main altar. According to the tradition of Saint James, the remains of the apostle are deposited there, recovered in the 19th century after nearly 300 years hidden beneath the flagstones of the Cathedral. In 1884 Pope Leon XIII declared that they belonged to the apostle. The Church thus aimed to close the still open debate about who really is buried in the Compostela sepulchre.

Silver sepulchral urn >

The chapels of the apse

The more than 15 chapels of the interior perimeter of the Cathedral reflect the variety of the catholic calendar of saints' days and a great diversity of artistic styles. Particularly attractive are the chapels located in the apse. Like on a stroll (in fact, this section is called "ambulatory"), the visitor can contemplate nine chapels, among them that of Salvador, the first to be built, in the 11th century, and that of Pilar, with an exuberant Baroque altarpiece.

Chapel of Mondragón

Chapel of Salvador >

The Holy Door

Chapel of Pilar >

Chapel of the Corticela

The chapel of the Corticela is one of the oldest areas of the Cathedral. When it was built in the 9th century it was a free-standing building, the oratory of the first monks. The current chapel is a later work, from the 12th century, but suggestive of the early structure. It is reached via a Romanesque portico with a tympanum on which is represented the Adoration of the Kings. Since the 16th century the Corticela has been the parish church of the foreign pilgrims.

The cloister

The cloister of the Cathedral is reached via the entrance to the museum. It is an architectural complex that was added in the 16th century, completing the perimeter of the Cathedral between the Praza das Praterías and the Obradoiro. The current cloister, in Renaissance style, was built at the behest of Archbishop Alonso de Fonseca, replacing the old 13th-century Gothic cloister.

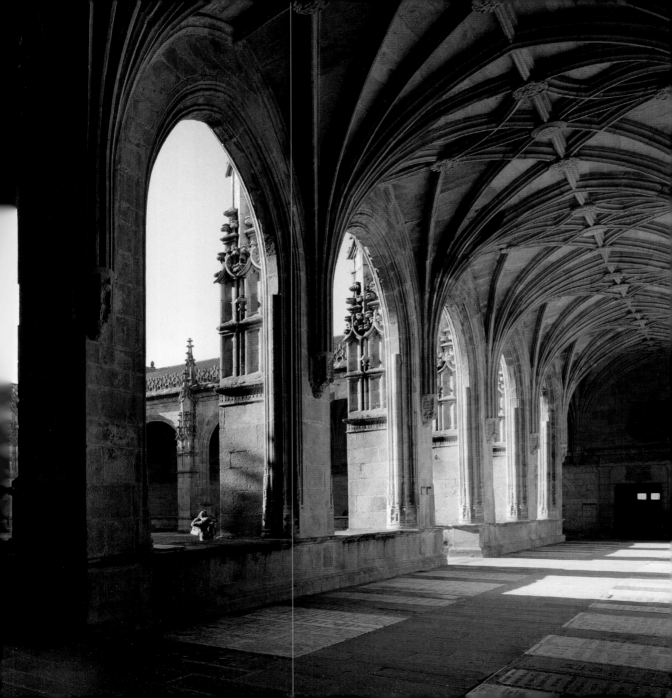

Chapel of the Relics, Royal Pantheon

Situated in one of the entrances of the Cathedral Museum it houses the sepulchres of the most powerful people of the period in which Galicia was a thriving kingdom in the far west of Europe. Resting in the Royal Pantheon are Raymond of Burgundy, Alfonso IX and Fernando II; Berenguela, wife of Alfonso VII, Juana de Castro and the Count of Traba. Until the 16th century the place was the old Chapter Room of the Cathedral.

Altarpiece of the Relics >

The Cathedral Museum

The recreation of the stone choir, the archaeological remains of the excavations in the Cathedral or the collections of gold and silversmithing and tapestries are some of the treasures of the Cathedral Museum. They are distributed in three spaces: the crypt, built by Mateo, the Treasury and the cloister. The first floor houses the Library and the Chapter Room, and on the top floor, the Halls of the Balconada, with a magnificent view over the Praza do Obradoiro.

Chapter Library, Cathedral Museum >

The Botafumeiro, thurible

The large thurible of the Cathedral, the Botafumeiro, is notable for its size (one and a half metres high) and its weight (53 kilos), but above all for the way it works. By means of pulleys and pushed by eight *tiraboleiros*, the Botafumeiro flies through the side nave to a height of 20 metres and a speed of 70 kph. It had a twofold function: liturgical and hygienic. It eliminated the unpleasant smells of the pilgrims who for one period of time slept inside the Cathedral.

The roof

The Cathedral of Santiago provides the possibility of reaching a privileged spot that normally only the cats enjoy: walking along the rooftop. The stone slabs that form the roof allow one to get a unique perspective of the building itself, the nearby squares and streets and the city as a whole. The roof is reached via the Gelmírez Palace by means of a twisting climb up the interior stairways of the Cathedral. The visit forms part of the Museum activities and is reached from the visitor reception centre of the Crypt and Glory Portico.

The Pazo de Raxoi

The building resting on arcades that occupies the whole western side of the Praza do Obradoiro is today the offices of the Ayuntamiento de Santiago, the town hall, and of the Presidency of the Xunta de Galicia. Built in the 18th century, it is known as Pazo de Raxoi, in memory of Archbishop Bartolomé Rajoy Losada. It is crowned by a sculptural series that represents the apostle in the legendary Battle of Clavijo. It was also a prison, seminary and residence of confessors.

Equestrian statue of Saint James >

Pazo de Raxoi, Praza do Obradoiro

Hostal de los Reyes Católicos

The Hostal de los Reyes Católicos was once a founding hospital. Built at the behest of the monarchs Isabel and Fernando to attend to the sick and pilgrims, it is now one of the principal hotels of the city. Despite the monumental character of the building, it is worth having a careful look at the details: the gargoyles, the filigree work of the cross vaulting of the oval chapel, the fountains of the interior courtyards, the stairways…

Adam and Eve

Gelmírez Palace

The Gelmírez Palace is in reality the second residence that the great medieval archbishop of Compostela had built. The first palace was situated towards Praterías and was destroyed in the popular uprising of 1117. In the current one we can still see the Romanesque portico and several singular spaces: medieval halls for festivals and banquets. On the outside, the Arco del Palacio covers the stairway that leads from the Obradoiro to Acibechería.

Corbels of the festival and dining hall >

Church of San Fructuoso

From the steps that drop from the Obradoiro to Rúa das Hortas, we can see the façade of the church of San Fructuoso, an 18th-century Baroque temple. Here stand out four figures that represent the four cardinal virtues: Prudence, with a mirror; Strength, with a column, Temperance, with a glass, and Justice, with a sword. Four figures that popular imagination identifies with the four Jacks of the Spanish pack of cards.

"The four Jacks"

College of San Xerome

The building with a Romanesque doorway that occupies the south side of the Praza do Obradoiro houses the the vice-chancellor's offices of the University of Santiago. The history of the College of San Xerome also coincides with that of the university itself. Its origin is found in the Estudio Viejo, a centre created by Alonso de Fonseca for poor students close to San Martiño Pinario. The Romanesque doorway comes from that original centre.

College of Fonseca

The thoughtful figure of Alonso de Fonseca overlooks, from the centre of the courtyard, the building with which the origins of the University of Santiago are identified. Created in 1495 by the notary Lope Gómez de Marzoa, Archbishop Alonso de Fonseca gave it its final impulse with the construction of the College of Santiago Alfeo, today known as the College of Fonseca. It currently houses the university library.

Medallions of the courtyard

Praza das Praterías

The Praza das Praterías is the smallest square surrounding the Cathedral, but condenses a large part of the architecture and history of Compostela society. From the façade of the Cathedral to the current Museum of Pilgrimages, work from the mid-20th century, the square is a merry amalgam of Romanesque; Renaissance, Baroque and contemporary elements. Some of the sculptures and reliefs of the Romanesque façade rival in beauty those of the Glory Portico, and the Renaissance medallions of the adjoining wall of the Cathedral, the wall of the cloister, attract one's attention facing the Baroque splendour of the Casa do Cabido. All of this is contained in a square overlooked by the impressive Clock Tower and by the stone eyes of the horses of the central fountain. The square that houses the Courthouse in the times of Gelmírez was also the place where the silversmiths of Compostela settled. The current jewellery shops of the square remind us of the traditional craftsmanship.

Detail of the Fountain
of the Horses

The Fountain
of the Horses

The scallop of Praterías >

The Casa do Cabido

How does one close off as beautiful a square as that of Praterías on the side facing the façade of the Cathedral? By building a large decorative set. This must have crossed the minds of those who, in the 18th century, decided to raise the Casa do Cabido. It is a veritable backdrop in stone with a clear decorative aim: the building is almost as narrow as the façade itself. The Casa do Cabido is a central monument of Compostela Baroque decorative architecture.

Torre Berenguela or Clock Tower

The Clock Tower, between Praterías and Quintana, is one of the major decorative projects of Compostela Baroque. Built by Domingo de Andrade in the 17th century, it stands 75 metres high from the foundations of an old defensive tower. The construction was complicated. Among other problems, the nuns of the convent of Antealtares complained that the height of the tower threatened their privacy. The clock was placed in the 19th century.

Praterías Doorway

The Praterías façade is the only one in Romanesque style conserved from the old design by Gelmírez. What we see now, however, is a large jigsaw puzzle with additions from the old Acibechería doorway. This almost fragmentary character gives it its great charm. The façade shares scenes of the temptations and the life of Christ with images of sirens, centaurs, zodiacal signs and David with his zither or the mysterious woman of the skull.

Figure of King David playing the zither

Museum of Pilgrimages

The building that frames the Praza das Praterías on the east is the most recent of the complex. Built in 1949, until 2004 it housed the offices of the Banco de España in Santiago. Today, after a thorough reform by the architect Manuel Gallego Jorreto, It hosts a part of the collection and activities of the Museum of Pilgrimages and Santiago, one of the new cultural and tourist facilities of the city.

Rúa de Fonseca

The street that connects the Praza das Praterías with the Obradoiro is Rúa de Fonseca, which also leads to the old offices of the university and Rúa do Franco. One can still visit old establishments that recall the splendour of the craft guilds and gold and silversmiths that worked around the Cathedral, particularly the silversmiths, jet workers and *cuncheiros*, who sold the Compostela scallop shells exclusively.

Rúa de Xelmírez

Arch of Xelmírez >

Praza da Acibechería

The numerous jet craftsmen workshops gave the square that opens the north façade of the Cathedral its name. Here arrived the pilgrims who travelled the ways that came from this direction, among them the most trodden, the French Way. The official name is, in fact, Praza da Inmaculada, although all the locals from Compostela know it by its traditional name. It is situated between the Cathedral and the imposing building of San Martiño Pinario, the former Benedictine convent and current Main Seminary. The church of the monastery is reached by a small alley, the Rúa da Moeda Vella, which keeps a small secret. It is the only street quoted with its current name in medieval Galician lyrical poetry, specifically in a canticle by Joán Vasques de Talaveira, a 13th-century minstrel. The Acibechería connects with the Praza do Obradoiro by the steps of the Arch of Gelmírez, a place where one can often hear the sound of bagpipes being played.

Main Seminary of
San Martiño Pinario

Acibechería Doorway

The Acibechería façade projects the Cathedral towards the north, and perhaps this is why it is the coldest and most sombre. Nothing remains of the old Romanesque doorway, although some figures were moved to the Praterías. What we now see is an 18th-century construction in the transition between Baroque and Neoclassicism. Entering through the door of the Acibechería we reach the chapel of the Corticela, a church inside a cathedral.

San Martiño Pinario

The monastery of San Martiño Pinario is one of the symbols of power of the Compostela church authorities. The current Main Seminary occupies a space of over two hectares and was built thanks to the income of the convent, with properties and rights all over Galicia until the mid-19th century. The church, reached via singular Baroque steps, houses a museum and an extraordinary altarpiece by Fernando de Casas y Novoa.

Monastery   Church of San Martiño Pinario >

Main Altar and choir, church of San Martiño Pinario

Rúa da Acibechería

From the Praza da Inmaculada leads Rúa da Acibechería, which in turn leads us to the Praza de Cervantes, the old market. The sale of objects made in jet, a variety of lignite, is documented in Compostela from the 13th century, and the jet workers guild was one of the most numerous and influential. The jewellery and souvenirs made with jet are still one of the most singular items on offer in the shops of the old quarter of Santiago.

Craftsman cutting jet >

Praza da Quintana

Plaque recalling
the Literary Batallion

From the steps that connect la Quintana de Mortos with that of Vivos, we can imagine what the Praza da Quintana was like in the Middle Ages. We see stands selling meat, fish and vegetables; oxen, sheep and pigs on show for sale; priests and monks from the Way, craftsmen's workshops, stone cutters who worked on the cathedral works always in progress... The current flagstone pavement did not exist, and all this activity was carried out on the land of the old graveyard, literally on the old tombstones. La Quintana, this singular vivid cemetery, was for centuries the economic and social centre of Santiago. From the plaque that recalls the Literary Batallion, made up of university students who fought against Napoleon, to the exhibition room of the Casa da Parra, the Praza da Quintana is also a venue for concerts, theatrical representations and social and political acts. It is a symbol of the civil heart of the city, the final journey of the pilgrim who arrives at the Holy Door along the Vía Sacra.

Royal Door, Praza da Quintana

Holy Door

The Holy Door is not opened with a key, but with a silver hammer that the archbishop uses on the 31st of December prior to a Jubilee Year to knock down the wall that seals the entrance. Unless one visits Santiago in a Holy Year, the Door will be closed by means of a large iron gate surrounded by 24 figures of prophets and apostles from the old stone choir built by Master Mateo. From the Holy Door we easily reach the crypt of the sepulchre.

Apostle Saint James (figure on the right)

Casa da Parra

The Casa da Parra is one of the best examples of Compostela civil Baroque. The work of the architect Domingo de Andrade, it gets its name from the bunches of grapes sculpted in stone of the façade. The upper balustrade and the top floor are recent, from the mid-20th century. When it was built in the 17th century, most of the houses in the city were made of wood, brick and thin walls. The building announces the stone Compostela of today.

Casa da Conga

The Casa da Conga is another large work planned by the architect Domingo de Andrade, although he died before seeing it completed. Used as the residence of the canons of the Cathedral, its construction meant the demolition of a large number of small homes and the unification into one single building all this side of the square. Its fourteen arches stand out, above which the façade is supported, and the large surviving chimney that crowns it.

Praza da Quintana, Medicine graduates

Tuna, student music group >

Convent of San Paio de Antealtares

The balustrade with pinnacles of the Cathedral contrasts with, on the other side of the Praza da Quintana, the sobriety of the large granite wall of the monastery of San Paio de Antealtares. A reminder of the early Benedictine cenacle, it is now a convent of cloistered nuns. The monastery church is reached via the Vía Sacra. In the entrance is a surprising image of Saint Pelayo, represented according to the story of his martyrdom in Cordoba, tortured and having his throat cut.

San Paio de Antealtares

2   The rúas

Strolling around the streets is the best way of discovering the old European cities. And Santiago is no exception: in fact it is a perfect example. When we walk around the old quarter of Compostela, we do so along streets formed in many cases 900 years ago: the Rúa do Franco, Rúa do Vilar, Rúa Nova, those which go from the Orfas to the Preguntoiro. Streets which start from (or lead to) the Cathedral like the side of a scallop shell. Over this old network, throughout the centuries homes and palaces, markets, theatres, taverns and hospitals were built, and all with a common element: granite stone. Granite on the façades, the arcades, the paving. The streets of Santiago form the petals of the "mystical stone rose" in the words of Ramón del Valle-Inclán. Streets connected by narrow alleys, such as that of Entrerrúas; discrete and solitary streets such as Rúa de Xerusalén, in contrast to the hustle and bustle of Acibechería and the Vía Sacra.

Rúa da Porta da Pena

1
Praza do Toural

2
Rúa do Franco

3
Rúa do Vilar

4
Rúa Nova

5
Praza de Cervantes

6
Praza de Abastos

7
Praza de Mazarelos

8
Rúa de San Francisco

9
Rúa da Acibechería

10
Rúa das Hortas

11
Church das Ánimas

12
Entrerrúas

13
Convent of Santa Clara

14
Casa da Troia

15
Church of Santa María Salomé

16
Church of Nosa Señora da Angustia

Praza do Toural

The Praza do Toural is one of the liveliest of the old quarter. At the intersection between the old part and the modern enlargement, it was at one time the place where the livestock market was held. The biggest building of the square is the Pazo de Bendaña, an 18th-century construction that today houses the Eugenio Granell Foundation. Over the central balcony is a statue of Hercules supporting the globe.

Statue of Hercules >

Rúa do Franco

Between the Praza do Obradoiro and the Porta Faxeira runs Rúa do Franco. We should clarify the origin of the name, which is none other than that of the pilgrims who reached Santiago via the French Way. It is the traditional street for drinking a glass of wine. Today its numerous restaurants have a varied gastronomic selection. It is well worth taking a look at the aquariums where the restaurant owners in Rúa do Franco display one of their star products: seafood.

O Gato Negro

Rúa do Vilar

If it rains you will have no problem strolling along Rúa do Vilar. Between the Praza do Toural and the Praza das Praterías we can walk along this street beneath the arcades of most of its houses. A real treatise about different types of arcade in one of the most charming streets of the city, with old-fashioned shops, cafés, urban palaces, art centres, small hotels and restaurants. The modern city with a medieval layout.

Arcades of the Rúa do Vilar

El Café Casino, in the Rúa do Vilar

Rúa do Vilar >

Symbols

Compostela is a city marked by time, nature and human activity. There sometimes exists a mysterious code of small urban details that appear unexpectedly before the eyes of passer-by; inscriptions on the lintels of small houses, scallop shells or stars sculpted in stone on the façades. Many simply point out the ownership of the property, but all together they create the subtle symbolic calligraphy of Compostela.

Rúa do Vilar

Rúa do Vilar

Ruela de Entrerrúas >

Rúa Nova

The Rúa Nova runs parallel to the Rúa do Vilar and it is easy to confuse the two. It also possesses many arcades and gives off this same stately air. Here was situated the College of the Irish and above it was built the Pazo de Ramirás. In the Rúa Nova are the Salón Teatro, home of the Centro Dramático Galego, and the Teatro Principal. A not-to-be-missed visit is the church of Santa María Salomé, one of the churches that Archbishop Gelmírez had built.

Arcades of the Rúa Nova ›

Praza de Cervantes

The Praza de Cervantes is another of the main intersections of the old city. It was the forum of the medieval city where the news and announcements of the City Council or archbishop were pronounced. Later, under the name of Praza do Campo, it was the busiest market of the city and the offices of the Council. The building that housed it is still conserved, situated on the corner that joins the Rúa do Preguntorio.

San Bieito do Campo >

Casa da Troia

Vía Sacra >

Santiago during festivals

In Santiago there are festivals for "indoors" and "outdoors". The "indoors" festival, the one that the people of Compostela celebrate themselves, is that of the Ascension, in spring. Dances, open-air celebrations, fine food, traditional sports… the ingredients of the city's most popular festival. The "outdoors" festival is that of the apostle, on the 25th of July, when the city celebrates for the visitors.

Festivals of the Ascension

The Praza de Abastos

Despite its medieval appearance, the Praza de Abastos is a work from the mid-20th century, built over an earlier project, from the previous century, in iron and glass. Situated between the church of San Fiz and the convent of Santo Agostiño, the farmers from round about still come to the Praza de Abastos to sell their produce. It is a perfect spot for taking in, buying or tasting some of the most typical products of Galician gastronomy.

Market of Abastos

Pulpo *á feira* (Octopus)

Praza de Mazarelos

The arch of the Praza de Mazarelos is the only doorway preserved of the old defensive wall of Santiago. As the plaque placed in the spot reads, here entered the muleteers who transported wine from Ulla and Ribeiro, and cereals from Castile. The arch opens into a square with the old building of the Faculty of Philosophy. From Mazarelos we reach the university church, attached to the Faculty of Geography and History.

Statue of Montero Ríos

Arch of Mazarelos >

Churches and convents

Santiago cannot be understood without the presence and influence of the Catholic Church. Nearly fifty temples and convents can be visited today. Apart from the cathedral, the oldest churches are those of San Fiz de Solovio, San Miguel dos Agros, San Bieito do Campo and Santa María Salomé. All of them date back as far as the mid-12th century. The commitment of the religious orders to Santiago is also clearly shown in their monasteries: the Benedictines of San Martiño Pinario, that of San Francisco and the Dominicans of Bonaval, without forgetting the convent of Santa Clara, with its Baroque façade crowned by a spectacular stone cylinder.

Convent of Santa Clara >

Nosa Señora da Angustia

Santa María Salomé

Church of Ánimas

Rúa de San Francisco

Many visitors, above all those who arrive in Santiago by coach, enter the Obradoiro by the Rúa de San Francisco. The first thing they see is the monastery of San Francisco, founded according to tradition by Francis of Assisi himself. The exterior features a sculptural series by the Galician artist Francisco Asorey. It is a curious street. On one side are small houses with shops, and on the other side, just two buildings: the imposing Faculty of Medicine and the side wall of the Hostal de los Reyes Católicos.

Church of San Francisco >

Rúa das Hortas

Going down the steps located between the Hostal de los Reyes Católicos and the Pazo de Raxoi, we reach the Rúa das Hortas, which means the street leading to the orchards, the rural area of the city. It is a way that winds its way between traditional houses, far from, yet still so close, to the monumentality of the central streets. The Rúa das Hortas shows us the close relationship between town and country that is still perceived in Compostela.

3   Outside the city

The old rural Compostela that surrounded the old walled city is now a close-woven belt of parks. From the Alameda to Belvís or the Pedroso, going through Bonaval, the estate of Vista Alegre or the park of Carlomagno, in the district of Fontiñas. Beyond the boundaries of the old centre also extends the area of new urbanism and contemporary architecture. It is almost a historical paradox, because for centuries the space for constructive intervention and experimentation was precisely the old part of the city. In the last thirty years new districts have been created, such as that of Fontiñas, or traditional districts were reformed, such as Conxo. Basic infrastructures of communication were built and access was improved. Also the institutions, such as the Xunta (Galician government), the Consorcio (City Council) or the University of Santiago, made a commitment to contemporary architecture for their new buildings of public use: from the Centro Galego de Arte Contemporánea to the Cidade da Cultura.

1
Cidade da Cultura de Galicia

2
San Domingos de Bonaval
Museo do Pobo Galego

3
Centro Galego
de Arte Contemporánea

4
Park of the Alameda

5
Park of Bonaval

6
Park of Belvís

7
Collegiate of Sar

8
Sarela

9
Park of Vista Alegre

10
Auditorium of Galicia

11
Ánxel Casal Library

12
Museum of Natural
History Luis Iglesias

13
Faculty of
Communication Sciences

Rúa do Pombal, with the Alameda in the background

The Alameda

How many photos have been taken from here? The Alameda provides the most well-known views of the city. Designed around the church of Santa Susana, the Alameda housed the Regional Exhibition of 1909, of which a building in Modernist style is conserved. It is also an area for festivals and open-air celebrations, and is the local people's favourite spot for chatting and strolling. It was the first public park in a city full of private gardens.

Avenue of Ferradura

Bandstand >

Statue of Manuel Ventura Figueroa

Dovecotes, Avenue of Ferradura >

Las Dos Marías, by César Lombera

Valle-Inclán, by Luis Miguel Bugallo

Church of Santa Susana, park of the Alameda

San Domingos de Bonaval

Since 1976 the convent of San Domingos de Bonaval has housed the Museo do Pobo Galego, the best place to discover the traditional culture of Galicia, from the trades relating to the sea and agriculture, to popular music and architecture. In the old convent you simply must see the triple spiral stairway, work of the architect Domingo de Andrade, and the Pantheon of Illustrious Galicians, where the remains of Rosalía de Castro and Castelao lay.

Convent of San Domingos

Sepulchre

Triple spiral stairway >

Museo do Pobo Galego, San Domingos de Bonaval

Centro Galego de Arte Contemporánea

It is located in the entrance of the park of Bonaval, just beside the Museo do Pobo Galego. Designed and built by the Portuguese architect Álvaro Siza, the CGAC has maintained a regular programme of exhibitions and activities since 1995. A large well-lit vestibule provides access to the halls, auditorium and library. It is the space that Compostela reserves for contemporary artistic creation.

Park of Bonaval

The gardens, stables and old cemetery were transformed into one of the most singular parks in the city. The architect Álvaro Siza conceived the project as a new public space between the convent of Bonaval and the Centro Galego de Arte Contemporánea. The result: a singular park, built on terraces, that conserves some old architectural elements: from fountains and ruins to the walls with niches of the old cemetery.

San Domingos de Bonaval

Belvís

It is one of the biggest recent parks of the city but is, however, difficult to see. It is located in a stream bed between the convent of Belvís and the Main Seminary, and the row of houses of the Rúa da Virxe da Cerca. The park can also be reached via the Rúa de San Pedro. It is an ideal spot for relaxing and doing sport, in which there are community gardening spaces, small urban allotments.

Rúa das Trompas >

Colegiata de Sar

Another hidden treasure on the city outskirts. Construction work on the collegiate of Santa María began in the 12th century and belonged to the Augustine order. Placed very close to the River Sar, the structure of the temple gave way and some solid buttresses had to be built to avoid it collapsing. Since then the walls and columns can be seen to be clearly inclined. It houses the Museo de Arte Sacro.

Church of Santa María de Sar >

Sarela

In the old Compostela everything is close by. Less than ten minutes' walk away from the Praza do Obradoiro via the Rúa das Hortas, in the direction of Monte do Pedroso, we come to an avenue in a natural setting on the banks of the Sarela, a tributary of the Sar. The route, recently fitted out, enables us to discover a hidden Compostela: that of the old mills and tanning factories, of narrow bridges and agricultural smallholdings.

Riverside Avenue of the Sarela >

Park of Vista Alegre

The old Simeón Estate is now the park of Vista Alegre or park of Europa, a space that conserves many of the aspects of stately gardens. Perhaps, however, what attracts our attention most are the new constructions: from the offices of the Estudios Avanzados y Altos Estudios Musicales to the Arteria Noroeste. A small Modernist palace was also reformed to become a residence for visiting university professors.

Casa Europa

School of Superior Musical Studies >

Museum of Natural History

Inside the park of Vista Alegre also stands the new building of the Museum of Natural History of the University of Santiago. Designed by the architect César Portela, the new facilities are designed to not only house the collections and the important scientific heritage of the university, but also offer these contents in an attractive and didactic way. A tour of the science produced in Galicia over the last 200 years.

Faculty of Communication Sciences

This faculty is another of the Compostela projects by the architect Álvaro Siza. Situated in the North Campus of the university, close to the faculty of Philology, it is one of the examples of contemporary urban intervention in Santiago. It is a building for training new journalists, a very recent addition to the qualifications attainable at the five-hundred-year-old Galician university.

Ánxel Casal Library

As well as the Xeral Library of the University of Santiago and that of the Cidade da Cultura, since 2008 Santiago has had a new reading space, the Ánxel Casal Public Library. Installed in a building by the architects Andrés Perea and Roberto Medín, it forms part of the network of nodal libraries of the Xunta de Galicia. It carries the name of Ánxel Casal, a publisher, pro-Galician, and Republican mayor of Santiago murdered in August 1936.

Auditorium of Galícia

It is one of the main cultural infrastructures in a city that is well-equipped for the creation and diffusion of artistic activities of all kinds. Home to the Real Filharmonía de Galicia, its two halls host a regular programme of music and all types of shows. It also has an exhibition room and a large cafeteria. The Auditorium is in the Parque de la Música, close to the university's North Campus.

Cidade da Cultura de Galicia

On the side of Mount Gaiás stand the undulating outlines of the Cidade da Cultura. It is a massive architectural complex designed by Peter Eisenman inspired by the layout in the form of a scallop shell of the old Compostela. The idea of those responsible for the project was to create a permanent tourist focus of attraction that would compensate for the discontinuous nature of the Jubilee years. Opened on the 11th of January 2011, the Cidade da Cultura is made up of four buildings, of the six planned, that house the Library, the Archive of Galicia, the Centro Gaiás Museum, the Creative Entrepreneurship Centre and the Cultural Innovation Centre. In 2013 the Xunta de Galicia halted work on the Theatre of Music and International Art Centre, the other two buildings planned in Eisenman's project. The Cidade da Cultura Foundation is responsible for the complex, which includes exhibitions, congresses and concerts throughout the year.

Centro Gaiás Museum

Creative Entrepreneurship Centre >

Santiago de Compostela
Literary landscape

There is a moment when every traveller who visits a new city asks themselves: what would it be like to live here? The Argentine writer Jorge Luis Borges said that, of all the cities he had known, Geneva seemed to him the closest to happiness. Perhaps this is the question we form subconsciously when we decide to set off on a journey: will there be any place especially disposed to be happy?

Walking around Santiago a similar question may arise. How does one live in a setting of stone and sky, of moss and rain? Are these men and women who cross, who stop and greet each other while calmly walking along the street happy? Obviously there is no single answer. How can we know whether we are living in a city or it is this city that lives through us? Each person will evaluate up to what point their happiness or otherwise is related to the place they were born or where they chose to live. The writer Ramón María del Valle-Inclán could not stand the clerical and provincial atmosphere of the early 20th-century Compostela, while others found the city and its environs suitable for study and literary or artistic creation. Even the scientific disciplines, from astronomy to chemistry, along with mathematics or cartography, achieved an early development in the Galician university. We just need to recall that the cloister of the faculty of History was illuminated one night in 1854 by the first electric light with voltaic arc ever to function in Spain.

However, the most popular image of the university and of Compostela in the early 20th century comes from *La Casa de la Troya*, the novel that Alejandro Pérez Lugín published in 1915. A recreation of this romantic and student atmosphere can now be seen in the House-Museum of the Rúa da Troia, one of the streets that lead off from the Rúa da Acibechería. The

Tuna, student musical groups, and Fonseca, "sad and alone", also form part of the image of Compostela, reinforced by the cinema. The novel by Pérez Lugín was adapted at least five times for the big screen, the first in 1924, directed by the author himself, and the last, a real success at the time, in 1959. Great directors discovered in Santiago the ideal setting for their films, from Luis Buñuel to Stanley Kramer. One of the most recent, the United States' actor of Galician origin Martin Sheen, produced a documentary about the Saint James Way called *The Way*.

Compostela has always been linked to faith, myth and legend. This is why the symbolic world has special significance in everything related to the city and the Way. Santiago and its stories are now sources of films, comics and video games, but for centuries Santiago was an eminently literary city, recreated and revealed through literature. From the Latin of the Codex Calixtinus to the Galician of the medieval troubadours, Santiago is present in the literature of the world's main languages. The poetess Rosalía de Castro, the woman who symbolised the renaissance (*Rexurdimento*) of Galician literature In the 19th century, was born in Santiago in 1837, and the entire city is full of her evocations: from the houses In which she lived to the large statue of the Alameda or the Pantheon of Illustrious Galicians in San Domingos de Bonaval, where her remains lay.

Rosalía de Castro is an excellent guide for a singular literary route that starts in Santiago and leads us to the Pobra do Caramiñal, In the Arousa estuary. The first stop is in Iria Flavia, this place of which Teodomiro was bishop and who in the 9th century discovered the sepulchre of Saint James. This town close to Padrón hosts the House-Museum of the Nobel Prize winner for Literature Camilo José Cela, who was born in Iria Flavia. Today, the collection of the Fundación Camilo José Cela Foundation, which Includes manuscripts and objects of the writer, is managed by the Xunta de Galicia in the Cidade da Cultura. Very close to the House-Museum of the Galician Nobel Prize winner, now in Padrón, is the House-Museum of Rosalía de Castro, where the foundation of the Galician writer promotes the study and diffusion of her work. Our next stop is in the seaside town of Rianxo, a little over 20 km from Padrón in the direction of Santa Uxía de Ribeira. This small town is the birthplace of three relevant figures from Galician culture: the politician, illustrator and writer Alfonso Rodríguez Castelao, one of the most outstanding figures of 20th-century Galicia; the

Country house in Oca,
A Estrada

Estuary of Muros and Noia

avant-garde poet Manuel Antonio, and one of the most singular writers of Galician and Spanish literature in exile, Rafael Dieste.

After visiting Rianxo, and in the same direction that we left Padrón, we reach Pobra do Caramiñal, the last place on this literary route. Although born in Vilanova de Arousa, on the other side of the estuary, Ramón del Valle-Inclán's family were originally from La Pobra, and here you can visit the museum about the writer, a space that also recreates the historical context where the early years of *Luces de bohemia* and *El ruedo ibérico* were developed by the author. Valle-Inclán died in Santiago de Compostela a few months before the outbreak of the Civil War and is buried in the cemetery of Boisaca in the Galician capital.

If the Cathedral of Santiago is the central axis of the city, Compostela is the compass around which revolves a large area of historic Galicia. The seafaring towns situated on the estuary of Muros and Noia until Fisterra, to where many pilgrims go to conclude their journey, seeing how the sun hides behind the Atlantic horizon. here are the country houses such as that of Oca, witnesses to the noble life of modern Galicia, or the medieval Benedictine monastery of San Lourenzo de Carboeiro, in the *concello* of Silleda, one of those extraordinary and almost secret monuments in the environs of Santiago.

When you return from your journey to Compostela perhaps you will come to think that the imagination of the men and women who built cities and paths from a dream is as solid as the stone of the streets and walls of Santiago.

Cemetery of Santa María a Nova, Noia

Fisterra

Santiago de Compostela
Galician gastronomy

Santiago cakes

It is often said that Galician cuisine is based on exceptional products: from the meat or vegetables to the fish and seafood. It is true. The climatic conditions of the country, from the continental climate of the interior mountains to the gently Atlantic climate of the Rías Baixas, and the wisdom of the men and women of the land and the sea favour the presence of magnificent products on Galicia's dinner tables. However, it is not enough to just have good ingredients to produce high-quality cuisine. Galician chefs have been able, above all in recent years, to present a top-class gastronomic repertoire at really competitive prices. Tradition and modernity on the tablecloths.

Pies

Octopus "á Feira"

It is the typical dish of festivals and processions, above all in inland Galicia. Cooked in large pots, the octopus is chopped with scissors and seasoned with salt, oil and paprika. It is served traditionally on wooden plates. In the estuaries, the octopus is prepared in *caldeirada*, with a garlic sauce and potatoes.

Peppers from Padrón

Excellent accompaniment for octopus and fish, these small peppers were introduced to Galicia from Mexico by the Franciscan monks of the convent of Herbón, in Padrón. They are fried in oil and, once out of the frying pan, seasoned with sea salt. You should be careful when eating them: there is always one that is really spicy.

Scallops

The scallop shell brings together love and the Way, Venus and Saint James. A symbol of the pilgrimage to Compostela, the interior of this mollusc is a delicate food and a real challenge for chefs. When its flavour and varied textures are achieved, the scallop is a subtle and delicious dish.

Seafood

The particular climatic conditions of the Galician coast favour the existence of an exceptional marine fauna: in both fish and crustaceans and molluscs. For centuries Galician cuisine specialised in the preparation of the best seafood, from the small crab or spider crab to the lobster or shrimp.

Shoulder of pork with turnip tops

The base of this traditional dish is the front trotter of the pig salted and cured, shoulder of pork and turnip tops, which are the tender leaves of the turnip cut before flowering. A reduced version of Galician stew, this dish of peasant origin can also be accompanied by Jerusalem artichoke and chorizo.

Galician stew

There was always a mug of stew in the country kitchens. It is a soup made from vegetables and potatoes cooked with some veal or pork lard. The stew was traditionally eaten after the main dish and not before, as is the custom nowadays.

Turnip tops

Meat "ao caldeiro"

It is a dish that is normally on the menu of restaurants serving traditional cuisine. The fact is that meat *ao caldeiro* suggests an ancestral way of preparing this product. The base of this dish is a good cut of veal, generally brisket, that is cooked with potatoes and served with salt and paprika.

The cheeses

The *tetilla* is most well-known, both for its shape and its taste. The variety of Galicia's cheeses, however, enable us to taste a whole range, from the smoked cheeses of San Simón da Costa to the delicate cheese of Cebreiro, in the mountains of Lugo, the place where the French Way enters Galicia.

National Livestock Market
of Amio